20

{ Advanced Communication

Tips for Couples }

Also by Doyle Barnett

20 Communication Tips for Couples:
A 30-Minute Guide to a Better Relationship

20 {advanced} Communication Tips for Couples

Doyle Barnett

Three Rivers Press
New York

A 90-MINUTE INVESTMENT IN A BETTER RELATIONSHIP

Published by Three Rivers Press, a division of Crown Publishers, Inc., 201 East 50th Street, New York, New York 10022. Member of the Crown Publishing Group.

Random House, Inc. New York, Toronto, London, Sydney, Auckland

http://www.randomhouse.com/

THREE RIVERS PRESS and colophon are trademarks of Crown Publishers, Inc.

Printed in the United States of America

Library of Congress Cataloging-in-Publication Data is available upon request.

ISBN 0-609-80031-0

10 9 8 7 6 5 4 3 2 1

First Edition

The Hindu say,
"When you're ready, your teacher will appear."

Most of what I know about couples' communication, I've learned from relationships past. This book is dedicated to all of those who've taught me by their love, their patience, and their tears.

Before we say anything to our mates, we need to ask ourselves:

"How is what I'm getting ready to say going to affect the way my mate feels about him- or herself?"

Contents

Acknowledgments 11

Foreword 13

Introduction 19

Tip 1 **Resolving Every Problem** 23
The dangers of letting a single problem go
unresolved

Tip 2 **Committing to Growth** 31
The necessity of committing to growing and changing

Tip 3 **Prioritizing the Moment** 37
Expanding our awareness of what is most important
during a conversation

Tip 4 **Establishing the Ambience** 47
How to prepare a safe environment so our message
will be received

Contents

Tip 5   **Clarifying Our Intentions**   53
Setting up the conversation to avoid putting our
partner on the defensive

Tip 6   **Setting the Tone**   57
Selecting the appropriate tone to best communicate
an issue

Tip 7   **Putting Feelings Before Facts**   63
Making the feelings we have for each other more
important than the issues

Tip 8   **Assisting Dialogue**   69
How to help our partner talk about difficult issues

Tip 9   **Disarming Our Mate**   75
Ways of getting our partner to answer our most direct
and personal questions

Tip 10   **Checking In**   83
Establishing regular updates with our mate to be sure
important issues are being addressed

Tip 11 **Full Disclosure** 89
Telling our mate everything we think they would
like to know

Tip 12 **Using Key Words** 97
Presetting specific code words that can't be misinterpreted

Tip 13 **Communication Contracts** 101
Making agreements that will be kept until it's time
to negotiate new ones

Tip 14 **Avoiding Absolutes** 107
Not allowing impassioned decisions to limit our
flexibility

Tip 15 **Reshaping Our Relationships** 111
Becoming aware of how our actions affect our
mate's perception of us

Tip 16 **Learning to Listen** 117
Learning why listening is more important for good
communication than speaking

Tip 17 **Softening Our Heart**   123
Learning to let down our defenses when we're
emotionally charged

Tip 18 **Repatterning Our Reactions**   133
Learning to recognize our negative reactions and
why we're so emotionally charged

Tip 19 **Comprehensive Communication**   141
Being complete and thorough enough in our
communications

Tip 20 **Walking Our Talk**   149
It's not what we know, it's if we're using what
we know

Acknowledgments

If it takes a whole village to raise a child, it's fair to say it takes a whole group to write a book. I'd like to express my appreciation to Lisa Byersmith, who helps me to walk my talk (my shining mirror); to David Krueger and Carrie Chong for their unconditional love and support (my best friends); to Rich Kot for his humor, patience, and technical support (he knows computers); to Dottie McIntosh and Fran Davis for their abilities to turn Ozarkian language into comprehensible text (my editors); and to Lesley Keenan for believing in my work (my agent).

Foreword

In this age of information, our access to new data increases daily. Success and personal growth favor those who have the ability to choose what is most applicable from the plethora of information available.

We feel guilty about our growing stacks of unread magazines. We wonder if we will ever find the time to learn all the software on our computers. And we worry that those college extension courses may be discontinued before we get a chance to take them. Being able to choose which learning resources will be the best investments of our limited time is the key.

For many of us, how well we do in our careers and in our personal lives is dependent on how well we are able to interact with other people and involve them in our ideas. Communication is a most important skill, one which will help us in our careers, as well as in our personal lives—communication not only with others, but also with ourselves.

People who spend years in countless classes, seeking to improve their professional skills and education, are often the same ones who avoid serious personal growth work because of the difficulty and frustration it causes them. On the other hand, some people are able to make deep personal changes and fully enjoy the process because they've developed the internal tools (the "personal-growth software") necessary for processing emotions and integrating positive changes.

With these internal thinking tools in place, personal growth and change are simply an enjoyable challenge rather than a task to be avoided.

It could be terrifying to be left alone on a 10,000-foot mountaintop in freezing weather, yet every year there are people who pay money for that experience. They enjoy testing their skills and the tools we call skis. The same attitude can exist for those who have acquired emotional-growth software. They enjoy the benefits of possessing communication skills and don't shrink from the challenge of testing their newfound relationships tools.

But where do we get such skills? Books, therapists, and workshop facilitators are one resource for personal-growth skills, but these avenues can be frustrating because it can be hard to clearly understand the information, and retention can be difficult without the tools to implement the changes.

What educators don't seem to know is that before they try to teach you new skills that will change your ways of thinking, they first need to give you the interface software needed to integrate that change.

Those who've avoided deep personal growth because they find it too difficult or boring would enjoy it if they first installed the proper tools for making internal changes. One such program for personal growth is our use of linguistics. If we want to change the way we think, then we first need to change the way we speak. Words are a major part of our human experience. We organize, define, and interpret our thoughts with words. How we think and feel about ourselves, about others, and about life is governed by the language we use.

The clearer our intrapersonal (internal) communications, and the broader our self-help vocabulary, the greater our ability to understand our experiences.

An example of how our linguistics styles either broaden or limit the way we think is so-called either-or thinking. When we see things as right or wrong, black or white, or good or bad, it confines us. Such absolute thinking restricts our interpretations of life and creates limitations that blind and frustrate us. The larger our self-help vocabulary, the more specific we're able to be and the clearer we are about our internal and external experiences. Speaking more articulately forces us to think more precisely. Greater precision provides us with more distinctions, hence more choices. When we see we have more choices available to us, we don't have to limit ourselves to this-way-or-that thinking.

If we learn from a counselor or a self-help book that we need to make some changes, such as getting more in touch with our emotions, we can look at it in two ways. If we view it with either-or thinking, we see either that they're wrong or that we're messed up. If we view the situation with more options, we still have a new challenge in this area of our lives that we need to overcome, but we get to use all the skills we've mastered in other areas of our lives to work on this temporary limitation.

By properly installing new interface software, we'll be able to integrate and implement any new information we receive about communication and relationships. With these new skills and thinking tools, we'll be able to have the fulfilling relationships that we've always dreamed of.

Of all input choices we have today, communication is the one skill that helps us the most. It helps us in dealing with others and is the most effective tool for emotional growth.

Introduction

Most of us haven't been exposed to many healthy, empowering relationships. Without healthy role models, we can only compare our "good enough" relationships to those that have bad or mediocre standards. We often refuse to see the possibility of a more fulfilling relationship with excuses such as:

- "My mate isn't interested in working on the relationship."
- "Every couple has their problems."
- "My career takes up most of my time and energy."
- "My parents are still together so their relationship must not have been so bad."

These forms of denial are common to those who've never experienced an exceptionally empowering relationship. Before we get too far into this book, I want to present a clear distinction between dysfunctional relationships and healthy ones.

Tips 1 and 2 are examples of this distinction. The couple in Tip 1 has the classical unsupportive relationship that we're all familiar with in one form or another. In contrast, the couple in Tip 2 are role models for those who've never experienced what true love can be like. They have one of those rare relationships to which we all aspire.

The rest of the communication tips are more advanced than those in my first book, but with patience and practice, you can master them as well.

If you've ever been lucky enough to know a couple in a truly fulfilling, intimate relationship, then you've had a glimpse of how high we can all set our standards. With the right tools and attitudes, we *can* achieve the same happiness for ourselves.

20

{ Advanced Communication Tips for Couples }

Tip 1

Resolving Every Problem

Tracy could tell when Craig woke up that he was having one of his headaches. She wanted to console him by letting him know that she understood how hard it would be for him to work all day with a migraine, but she said nothing. Experience told her that if she offered sympathy and listened to his complaints, sooner or later he would get off on a tangent, and his complaints would ultimately end up being about her.

Tracy noticed that Craig often blamed her for his own inability to deal with problems. He claimed his migraines were due to a lack of sleep caused by her restless tossing, or he would blame her for his impatience when she was running late. He always seemed to be trying to improve something about her. Craig complained about her driving, her cooking, even the way she dressed.

Tracy resented him for his faultfinding, so she seized every opportunity to point out when she was right, which led to more friction between them. Tracy knew that her husband loved her but she didn't think he liked or accepted her for who she was.

In spite of his headache, Craig started to make the bed but stopped when he remembered that he had made it for the last two mornings. He was tired of carrying more than his share of the load. Before they married, Craig went out of his way to help Tracy. He loved pleasing her but he soon realized that she enjoyed receiving more than giving.

Craig knew he wasn't a tit-for-tat type of person, but he felt their give-and-take was out of balance. Tracy would do a few things for him and then think they were equal. Sometimes she expressed her appreciation for what he did, but to keep things in balance, Craig needed her to *show* her appreciation by giving to him and their relationship as much as he felt he did.

When Tracy first noticed problems in their relationship, she sat down with Craig to discuss the issues. Then she realized that she was always the initiator of discussions and that Craig didn't keep the agreements he made. He seemed unwilling to work on the relationship even though he often complained about it.

They discussed counseling, so Tracy did some research and passed on to Craig the names of several counselors with good reputations. When he failed to follow through, Tracy felt defeated. She thought that Craig didn't care enough about their relationship to be willing to get help. She remembered their earlier happiness and wondered how their relationship had gotten so off track.

Craig accepted that all couples had disagreements. In the past when he had an argument with a girlfriend, they would stick with the discussion until they had resolved all their ill feelings. With Tracy, however, there was never any resolution, and Tracy would ignore the topic until it surfaced again as the same unresolved problem. Craig was tired of dealing with the same problems over and over, so he began to avoid discussions. His experience was that discussing their problems caused more stress than the problems themselves. He knew he was lowering his standards, but he told himself that no relationship was perfect.

Like most unhealthy couples, Craig and Tracy are caught up in a pattern of resentment and action-reaction. When couples don't completely address issues as they arise, the issues turn into problems. As problems continue, we build up resentments. And instead of *acting* out of love, we find ourselves *reacting* out of resentment.

We need to build give-give relationships, where we appreciate our

mates so much we aren't able to do enough to show them our grati-
tude—unlike Craig and Tracy, who have a take-take relationship where
they both end up feeling taken for granted or taken advantage of.

Often we let so many problems go unresolved we feel too over-
whelmed to deal with them. Then our stored-up ill feelings overpower
our feelings of love. The magic disappears, yet we stay together even
though we're unfulfilled.

> We need to become more committed to happiness or per-
> sonal growth than we are to commitment.

If we realize that our standards for a happy relationship have degener-
ated, we have some decisions to make. Are we going to do nothing and
settle for less, or are we committed to having a fulfilling relationship?

Are we going to let things continue and hope they'll get better, or are we going to actively deal with each problem one by one until we have the empowering relationship we've always wanted?

Tip 2

Committing to Growth

Vicki knew Ted was having a hard time at his job. Although he had agreed to repaint the porch during the weekend, she chose not to mention it. She knew if she did, he would feel bad about not keeping up with his chores. His feelings were more important to her than the porch. She wanted Ted to be happy and to enjoy their marriage, so she tried not to say or do anything that would sound unaccepting of him or his problems.

For the past two months Ted had been ordered to work late. He apologized to Vicki for being gone so much. Although he knew she understood, he still inquired how she felt about it. Ted knew that giving Vicki a chance to express her feelings would help her to better accept his absence. They both agreed there wasn't much he could do about the demands of work, and he reassured her that he understood her frustration and anger, even when it was directed at him. He cared about and understood her feelings, even when they weren't always rational.

From past experience, Vicki knew that she could trust Ted to give their relationship priority over any issue that arose. Ted wanted the best possible relationship with Vicki, so whenever a problem came up, even the smallest issue, he talked to her about it. More important, they continued to work on it until it was completely resolved. If talking wasn't enough, they sought help from a counselor.

Vicki cared enough about Ted and their relationship to handle any ill feelings that could potentially raise even the slightest barrier between them. She knew the situation at Ted's work could last for a while. She also knew their relationship and happiness were controlled by the two of them, not by his work. Vicki understood that their marriage would be happy as long as they gave each other's feelings priority over any issues that arose.

When others comment about how happy this couple is, they don't realize that either Vicki or Ted could be happy alone or with a different mate. Vicki and Ted do have the ideal, healthy relationship that most couples want, but what makes it ideal isn't their chemistry, their similarities, or even the depth of their love—it's their attitude toward their relationship and their commitment to personal growth.

This attitude of appreciation, and willingness to grow and change, is the source of their joy. They've also made the commitment to always establish feelings as a priority—their feelings about themselves, about each other, and about the relationship. They both know the golden rule:

> If we want our mates to love us, then we need to be sure they feel good about themselves whenever they're around us.

The essential goal Ted and Vicki share is to say or do nothing to trigger feelings in their mate that will cause that person to feel bad, unaccepted, or "less than" in any way. They're both committed to being aware of, and to dealing with, all unwanted negative or destructive feelings. They've stopped nagging, resenting, competing, and complaining about each other.

Ted and Vicki know communication is the key to dealing with feelings—communication with each other and within themselves. They also know that committing to growing and changing is essential to a happy life and relationship.

Tip 3

Prioritizing the Moment

Sheri was meeting her boyfriend Andy for their weekly lunch at a local restaurant, even though they had argued on the phone the night before. As she sat down, Sheri felt butterflies in her stomach. She suspected that Andy might be resentful because of the things she'd said to him on the phone. Lunch was a lot of small talk and uneasy laughter. Sheri wanted to talk about their recent disagreement, but decided the restaurant wasn't the place to bring up a potentially inflammatory subject. Both acted as if the argument had never happened. After lunch there was an awkward good-bye hug, and they parted feeling miserable and sad, with neither knowing what the other was thinking.

By the time they met two days later for a drive out of town, Sheri had prepared herself for the worst—the breakup she thought Andy was sure to suggest. All of Sheri's defenses were up. She was impatient, short-tempered, and oversensitive with Andy. He interpreted this as a signal that Sheri was ready to break up, and he reacted accordingly. When they were finally able to talk about their argument, so much new fear and anger had been generated that they were barely able to reconcile.

Sheri could have avoided those damaging feelings if she had "prioritized the moment." If at the restaurant she had taken an inventory of what issues most needed to be addressed at that time, she would have seen that her fears and reactions were emotionally separating her from Andy.

Had she told Andy how she felt about their previous argument, it would have eased some of their bad feelings. If Sheri had said to Andy in a loving tone, "I feel sorry about some of the things I said last night and I hope we can talk about it later when we're on our trip," it would have reassured Andy that she still cared about him and their relationship. He, in turn, could have taken the opening to briefly say how he felt, reassuring Sheri of his commitment.

Bringing an uncomfortable topic out in the open, even briefly, is often enough to take some of the charge from the situation and provide an opportunity for reconnection. We tend to avoid uncomfortable topics, particularly during times of stress, thinking we'll only make matters worse. This avoidance is valid in public or formal settings—or when the topic is used for nagging, with no immediate intention of addressing the issue. However, whenever there is a charged issue that is causing discomfort between two people, it's best to at least mention it. We must let our mates know we're concerned and that we want to talk about it when an opportune time arrives.

The most important issues to address, the ones that should always take precedence, are the feelings that are present in any caring situation.

It's important how our companions are feeling at that moment. If they feel angry, hurt, or afraid, then at the least, it should be mentioned right away.

When we're not accustomed to discussing our feelings, doing so can be uncomfortable or frightening, but our fears do tend to exaggerate problems. How often have we finally talked to our partners only to find that they weren't as upset as we had imagined?

We've all met poor communicators, people who are sincere but whose conversation and interactions with others are inappropriate. There are also those who may show little restraint, like children or older people. For example, I recently met an old man at a bus stop. His first words to me were, "My daughter is upset with me." Instead of a suitable greeting, he chose to express a random personal thought that was out of context to the situation. His awareness didn't extend far enough beyond himself to appropriately address me or the setting we were in.

Instead of prioritizing the moment, which is looking at the big picture and placing discussion topics in perspective, poor communicators will avoid uncomfortable issues or talk about themselves or their needs. They seem to be unaware of the needs and desires of others, or the current requirements of the relationship.

Another example of people who don't prioritize the moment are those who talk too much. Such people don't understand why others accuse them of incessant babble, because in reality they don't talk *any more* than anyone else does. However, they seem to talk "to" or "at," and not "with" others. They drone on and on, without checking in with their listeners to see if what they are saying is of any interest. If incessant talkers searched for feedback while speaking, they could tell if their listeners were interested in what they were saying. If they prioritized the moment, they would discover that their listeners weren't enjoying the conversation. They could then modify their behavior by changing the topic, asking questions, or giving their listeners a chance to talk.

A final example of poor communicators are people who use humor as a way to avoid intimacy. Instead of being in the moment and addressing the feelings that are present, such people make jokes to lighten the mood or avoid the topic.

Joe, a friend of mine, is an excellent communicator. In his interactions with others, he's constantly taking inventory of the issues that need to be addressed at the moment. He recognizes others' feelings and acknowledges what the status of his relationship with them is.

Once I ran into Joe at a restaurant. He had promised a few weeks earlier to give me some work-related materials but had yet to deliver them. Since our friendship was new at that time, he didn't want me to think he cared so little for me that he would forget about his promise. Joe immediately apologized for his failure. He was embarrassed to have to mention his lack of responsibility, but decided it was better than having me believe he didn't care about our friendship.

If Joe suspects that a charged issue could exist between him and someone else, he makes a point of mentioning the issue in a way that assures the other person of his concern. He mentions the problem as soon as appropriately possible, thus preventing uneasy feelings from magnifying until there's an opportunity to discuss the matter in detail.

Prioritizing the moment isn't expressing everything we think or feel without regard for other people's needs—but it is placing important feelings uppermost on our agenda.

Tip 4

Establishing the Ambience

Brian wanted to talk to Jude about the way she was treating him, but he was afraid she would react defensively and he would just make things worse between them. Whenever he tried to explain how her behavior was affecting him, she became angry or hurt. It would take days before the uneasy feelings went away. The more he tried to talk to her, the worse her reactions became.

Sometimes Brian would wait months before he brought the subject up. He hoped that time would heal her sensitivity about that issue, but no matter how long he waited, she was still too reactive to discuss her behavior toward him.

When we want to discuss a sensitive issue with our partners, we need to first prepare a safe environment so our message will be received. We can establish a secure ambience by tapping into the feelings of love and trust we share with our companions. In a sincere voice, we need to remind our partners how much we care about them and about our relationships.

We must assure our mates that their feelings are more important to us than the issues we want to discuss.

By first tuning in to our mates and connecting with the good feelings we share, we can often change whatever mood they're in and prepare them to hear what we have to say.

If we blurt out our thoughts and concerns without first being reassuring and connecting to our partners' feelings, we can expect only defensiveness from them. In order to receive our message, our mates must have open hearts and open minds. If they feel attacked in any way, they will put up their defensives and be closed-minded to whatever we say. If we begin conversations with statements such as "You had better listen to me this time" or "I'll say it again, you don't _____" or "And another thing you do is _____," then our companions won't feel safe enough to be receptive to what we have to say.

If instead we set the mood by telling our mates how important they are to us, we can then say something such as "I feel a little sad because there are some things I'd like to discuss with you but I don't know how to start" or "Is there anything I can do to help you feel comfortable enough to talk about _____?" or "I need your help with a problem that I have."

Each of these statements establishes an ambience of sincerity. If said in a proper tone to a trusting listener, there's less of a chance to trigger any defenses that would block communication. If our message is important, we need to take the time to set up the conversation in a sensitive manner.

Tip 5

{ *Clarifying Our Intentions* }

Allison was anxious when her boyfriend Rodney announced he was coming over to discuss something important. They weren't getting along very well and Allison was afraid that Rodney was going to break up with her.

When Rodney arrived, they sat outside near the pool. Rodney began by saying how much he liked her and how much he had enjoyed their times together. As he talked, Allison's fear increased. She suspected he was trying to make her feel better so he could let her down more easily, so she didn't listen very attentively. She held her breath, preparing for those crushing words: "Let's just be friends." She was also busy planning her rebuttal.

Rodney explained how busy he'd been since he started his new job. He finally apologized for the way he had been neglecting her, and asked her if she now understood why. Allison couldn't answer him. She had been rehearsing all the things she was going to tell him and had barely heard a word he said. She was relieved, but had been so defensive she was unable to appreciate his vulnerability or hear his painstaking explanation.

When Rodney first suggested getting together for a talk, he could have let Allison know what his intentions were. He didn't need to deliver his message over the phone, but he could have hinted that he was happy with her or that he was looking forward to spending more time together. Allison would have been more receptive to his message and it would have been a kind thing to do, considering the fragility of their relationship.

We need to have a special regard for our mates' feelings when there are sensitive issues to be discussed.

We can inform them of our intentions before we begin our conversation. If, like Rodney, we have to schedule a sensitive talk in advance, we must let our companions know the purpose of our discussion so they can emotionally prepare themselves.

We must learn to clarify our intentions to our mates as soon as we are aware of them.

Tip 6

Setting the Tone

Chad had been arguing with Joanne for several weeks. He'd tried many times to tell her how much he loved her, but every time they spoke she'd cry and send him away. Chad couldn't understand what was upsetting her. He carefully chose and rehearsed his words ahead of time so he'd be sure not to say the wrong thing, yet she still acted hurt.

What Chad didn't realize was that although his words said he loved her, his tone and body language communicated something else.

The specific words we choose when we speak are very important. However, studies have shown that words themselves only account for 7 percent of the message that is received. The other 93 percent of our communication is done through tone and body language. Most of what we communicate is received subconsciously.

We may say all the right things, but if we say them in the wrong tone our message may not be heard. Tone is much more than just the sound of a voice; it's also the perceived attitude, intentions, and emotions behind the words.

When a good friend jokingly calls us a fool, it means something much different than if someone we dislike calls us the same thing. It isn't the words that matter as much as the manner in which they are spoken.

When talking to our companions, we need to constantly be aware of the tone of our voice, the communication our body language reveals, and the overall impression of our message.

If our partners sense feelings of hostility, anger, or resentment from us, they most likely will not hear the words we speak, even if those words are supportive and kind.

The opposite is also true. If our partners experience love, acceptance, and sincerity in our voice and body language, we can say critical things without triggering reactions such as anger, hurt, or defensiveness.

Tone is the emotional sense that's created during a conversation. Tone can convey compassion, blame, or even urgency. Often, our message isn't heard correctly because we don't set the proper tone.

How many times have we tried to tell our partners that a topic is important to us, only to have those words fall on deaf ears? In these instances we need to set the proper tone by saying in a firm voice, "I'd like to talk to you about something important, so I need your full attention." This sets a tone of seriousness.

Before speaking to our mates, it's important to remember that it is we who have the ability to establish the tone for the conversation. If we're upset and we begin with accusations and insensitivity, our companions will respond in the same manner—unless we're fortunate enough to have an emotionally mature mate who can deflect our hostility and respond to us with love and compassion.

When we want to establish a tone of acceptance, our voice and body language must be softer. We need to sit close to our mates, and gently touch them if that feels appropriate. We can even suspend our disapproval of what our companions are saying until they have a chance to *fully* express themselves. We must be open to their statements or opinions even when we don't accept them. When our partners see that we seem to be accepting what they are saying without pouncing on them, they will open up even more and true communication can happen.

At first, pretending to accept our mates' statements may feel dishonest; however, we soon realize that by not reacting defensively, we're able to be more accepting of them and our general tone softens automatically.

Like many of these tips, this one can also be used to abuse our mates. The tone of a casual insult, delivered in a joking manner, may sound playful, but the real meaning behind the words is degrading. It's important not to use this tip as a tool for passive aggression.

Setting the proper tone is a surprisingly effective tool that's essential to good communication.

Tip 7

{ *Putting Feelings Before Facts* }

Art just can't understand why Kathy gets so upset when they disagree about something. He doesn't raise his voice or get angry. He doesn't even need to be right all the time. He simply tries to be logical and discusses the issues in order to find a solution to their dispute. Yet whenever they have a serious conflict, Kathy becomes so frustrated she cries and Art can't understand why.

> Kathy: *"I just don't like you going to those business conventions in Las Vegas."*
>
> Art: *"Do you still think I slept with one of those escorts we hired last year?"*
>
> Kathy: *"I don't know."*
>
> Art: *"We've already been over this, and you agreed that nothing happened."*

Kathy: "I know."

Art: "Your brother was with us. He told you I didn't do anything wrong."

Kathy: "I would still rather you didn't go."

Art: "Kathy, I'm telling you, you have no reason to worry
about me. Your brother and his wife will be with me this
time."

Kathy: "They can't be watching you all of the time."

❖   ❖   ❖

This dispute will end in the same way all of their prior ones did. Kathy
will be crying and Art will have no idea what he did wrong.

In spite of all his good intentions, Art truly isn't listening to Kathy.

Whenever she tells him how she feels he tells her why she needn't feel that way. He tries to convince her that her unwanted feelings are caused by misinformation.

> We need to place more importance on feelings than we do on facts.

Art gets impatient because Kathy can't give a logical argument why he shouldn't go to Vegas again. Whether Kathy can trust him in Vegas or not isn't the most important issue here. What's most important is the very fact that Kathy *feels* insecure and that she feels she can't trust him. Art's concern that she can't trust him this time in Vegas is misplaced. The important issue here is that she mistrusts him at all. If Art genuinely cares about Kathy and about having a healthy relationship, he would be more concerned about her feelings and her loss of trust in him than about whether he did something wrong or not.

Art needs to find out the underlying reasons Kathy feels insecure. Is it just a problem she has, or has he done something to trigger her doubts about him?

It is important during an argument to help minimize misunderstanding by recognizing the facts. However, the feelings that each person has, justifiable or not, are just as vital to maintaining the love and trust that is needed to keep a healthy relationship growing.

When discussing an issue, it's equally as important to explore the sources of each other's feelings as it is to examine the facts.

Tip 8

Assisting Dialogue

Soon after Barry arrived home from work he noticed that Lynn was unusually quiet. He asked her several times if everything was okay and she assured him it was, but Barry could tell something was bothering her.

Although Lynn was a third-generation American-born Chinese, she had been raised with an Asian sense of privacy and often found it difficult to discuss personal matters even with her husband.

Barry finally confronted her in bed that night and begged her to tell him what was going on. Lynn cried for over an hour. When she tried to speak, the tears welled up again and she shook her head in silence.

Days later Barry found out that Lynn had been diagnosed with breast cancer and was too ashamed to talk about it.

❖   ❖   ❖

Occasionally, in conversations with our mates a topic or situation will arise that is too difficult or painful for them to talk about. Fear, anger, or shame can carry such emotional charges that they are unable to communicate their feelings, or to even speak coherently.

Our mates may even attempt to tell us how they feel, but find speaking too difficult. When they clam up, we're unsure how to respond.

Along with the disarming techniques in Tip 6, another tip that often works to assist people who're having difficulty talking is to make verbal guesses about the cause of the upset. If we don't get a response with our first guess, then we need to guess again and again, much like the game Twenty Questions. Usually if our guess is close enough to the problem, we'll get a reaction. Then we can continue to zero in on the problem until we get close enough that our mates are able to start talking about it.

Barry could have asked Lynn: "Are you upset about something I said or did?" If no response, then: "Did something bad happen to you or a friend today?" or maybe: "Did you hear some bad news about something?" Barry could continue with the questions until he gets a response from Lynn. Most likely if his guesses get close enough, she will respond.

This technique works because mentioning a potential problem, saying it out loud, breaks the ice and takes some of the charge off the issue.

> When our mates hear us mention the problem out loud, they realize that the topic is neither unthinkable nor unspeakable after all.

We can also help our companions answer difficult questions by incorporating the answer within the question itself. A simple yes or no answer can be easier for them to verbalize than discussing a sensitive subject.

Another way we can assist our mates with communication is to assure them that we care about their feelings and that we're there for them no matter what the problem is. We can promise that whatever they reveal will be kept private and that we'll never bring up the subject again unless they speak about it first. We can also let them know that we're open to exploring any areas where we may be at fault.

These techniques will assist our mates in opening up channels of communication with us. They'll help to build trust if they're used properly—because we care, and not because we want to get information that can be used against them. When our companions open up to us, they're putting their hearts in our hands. We need to be gentle and take extra care with our words.

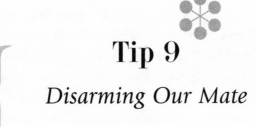

Tip 9

Disarming Our Mate

Becky dated Victor several times. She liked him, but she had the impression that he wasn't as interested in her as she was in him. They had just returned from a dance and Becky was feeling more insecure than ever. Although they'd both danced with others, Victor had danced repeatedly with a woman named Marsha. He even danced the last dance with her. Out of self-protection, Becky wanted to know if Victor was interested in Marsha. But she felt too embarrassed to ask, because she and Victor had made no commitments to each other. She feared he might stop dating her if he thought she was growing possessive or jealous, yet she didn't want to continue investing her emotions in him if he was interested in another woman.

How often have we had doubts or questions about our partners, but hesitated to ask because we were afraid of offending them or hurting their feelings? Even though the information we want may not be such a deep dark secret, some things can be difficult to ask and difficult for our companions to reveal. With special care, there are ways to disarm our mates and help them discuss sensitive issues with us.

For many of us, communication is the most difficult when we feel we are wrong in some way, like Becky's fear of being too attached. We don't want others to discover our weaknesses, our humanness. Deep down, however, we all want to be accepted for who we are. When we find someone who can accept us in spite of our faults, we're relieved of the burden of insecurity. Then and only then can we reveal our hidden imperfections.

If we suspect that our mates will have a difficult time disclosing something to us, then we must approach them in such a way that will minimize their defenses—a way in which will let them know that we will accept them no matter what they reveal to us. Our questions should be phrased to let them know that we will accept them no matter what they divulge.

For example, we might suspect our mate of having locked the key inside the car again—in spite of our warnings to get a spare key made. Their tendency would be to hide from discovery to avoid a lecture. If we ask, in a lighthearted and humorous tone, a question such as "Did your car lock you out again?" it may be easier for them to answer honestly. In a joking way this approach points the blame at the car rather than at them. Our tone and humor imply that we aren't making a big deal out of the situation.

Disarming questioning is a way of phrasing questions so that they don't alarm, frighten, or antagonize our mates. If we can master this, then we can help them disclose personal details about themselves which they have never been able to tell anyone else. We could even ask our mates if they were tempted to have sex with someone else. If they hear acceptance in our voice and they believe that we're understanding and nonjudgmental of them, they're much more likely to reveal even deeply private secrets.

Another tip for disarming is a form of "normalizing," letting someone know that we don't think the topic, or questions about it, are abnormal in any way.

> With normalizing, we can get answers to very direct, potentially embarrassing questions, so long as our tone is sincere.

As an example: We notice that the woman in the seat next to us on a plane has a split lip and a black eye. We could ask her if her husband hit her. After her initial surprise, she would see that we're being sincere and would be able to answer the question honestly.

Becky could have asked Victor about his attraction to Marsha without making him uncomfortable or without his suspecting that the subject was a charged issue for her. She could have set the conversation up by talking about the dance or dance partners, and carefully introducing Marsha's name. Then, in an easygoing tone, she could have asked, "Do you think there is any chance that Marsha could be your type?" By using this nonchalant tone, Becky not only tells Victor that it's not a big deal for her, but she also hints that she's on Victor's side and hopes that he may have a "chance" with Marsha.

If our mates are able to confess their infractions, we must then decide which is more important to us: having their trust and openness, or using the opportunity to pounce on them for their behavior. We must also decide if it's fair to use this information against them in the future. These decisions are determined by the level of trust and openness in a relationship.

Learning to disarm our mates is a valuable tool that can open up many areas of communication by developing responsibility, trust, and sensitivity to each other.

Tip 10

Checking In

How often have we heard statements like these? "She broke up with me out of the blue." "I couldn't believe it when he said he has been unhappy with our relationship for years." "I had no idea she was still upset about our anniversary last year."

All of these statements reveal a lack of communication on both people's part. If these couples had practiced "checking in" with each other on a regular basis, these painful surprises wouldn't have occurred.

Checking in is monitoring our relationships. It's a regular checkup that helps us to tune into what is really going on with our partners. It's questioning our companions about how they are feeling: about us, about themselves, about our relationship, about an issue, or about an event. It's also informing them about how we feel concerning any of these issues. It's an opportunity to keep the relationship clear of any undesired feelings, such as anger, guilt, or suspicion, and it also gives us a chance to become aware of any reactions going on such as defensive-ness, resentment, or insecurity.

At the first opportunity we get in our current relationship, we need to start checking in. We can ask our mates about how it has been so far, how it is now, and how they see the relationship in the future. We can ask them whether we have said or done anything that has made them feel uncomfortable in any way and, if so, how they would like us to act differently in the future. We need to make a habit of creating this oppor-tunity to clear up all unsettled feelings and misunderstandings. We can anticipate any potential issues and possibly prevent them from becom-ing problems.

Checking in is especially good to do after an argument. We can inquire as to how our partners are currently feeling about the disagree-ment. We need to find a way for us to feel good about ourselves, about our relationship, and about each other. If we let even one unsettled feeling reside, it could undermine the good feelings we have for each other. If we allow these unsettled feelings to add up, they will eventually outweigh the good feelings we have for each other and emotional separation will result. We can use our arguments as opportunities to learn more about our companions.

> We need to probe deep into each other's feelings, searching
> for any possible signs of residual resentment that could
> potentially cause problems in our relationships.

We need to use every argument with our partner as a stepping stone in our relationship rather than a stumbling block.

It's particularly important to check in during, or at least soon after, a stressful situation such as a disastrous vacation, a career change, or any important event that could affect us, our mates, or our relationships. It's best if we check in with each other *before* a stressful situation occurs. We can discuss ahead of time what is expected of us and the best way to handle it. We need to make it a habit to continue checking in on a daily basis for the rest of our relationship.

We can't assume that because everything appears fine to us, it's okay with our partners. They may be having a hard time trying to tell us something. We also need to learn to check in with ourselves to be sure we have no stored-up ill feelings. We can't allow the sun to set on any issue that could potentially undermine the trust we have established in our relationship.

Tip 11

Full Disclosure

Autumn was very attracted to Wayne. She wanted to continue dating him, but was afraid that if he found out about her temper before he got a chance to know her better, he would end the relationship. She also concealed her disgust with his smoking habit.

They dated for a few months and fell in love. After a while, Autumn discovered that Wayne was afraid to open his heart to her. She accused him of being the typical male, afraid of intimacy. What Autumn didn't realize was that Wayne couldn't be open and vulnerable with her because he didn't trust her. She had concealed her thoughts and feelings from him so often, he had no way of knowing what she was actually like.

One tool to help build trust, honesty, and friendship is full disclosure: telling our mates everything they need and want to know about our habits, thoughts, fears, and suspicions.

Some years ago, I conducted a survey of couples who had been married more than fifty years. Most couples claimed that trust was the most important factor in sustaining a healthy marriage. While many couples say they trust each other, there's more to trust than just feeling secure that our mate won't have an affair or leave us for another. Trust is knowing that our mate cares more about us than about the relationship. It's knowing we don't have to compete with our mates to get our needs met because they will always take our needs into consideration when making a decision.

> We need to develop a trusting relationship that is based on openness rather than concealment.

We reason that if we don't disclose our past mistakes or reveal our current flaws, doubts, or fears, we'll be easier to love; we believe our partners will think more highly of us and trust us more. On some level, however, as with Autumn and Wayne, our mates will know when we're holding back and it will erode their trust in us. Out of self-protection, our companions will have to imagine what we're not telling them—and imaginary problems are often worse than real ones.

Screening out the truth, and pretending to accept everything about our current mate, are obstacles to building real trust. To create solid, lasting trust, we must found our relationships on total honesty and openness. Trust is created only when our partners know we're disclosing everything—our past and present weaknesses and insecurities as well as our strengths. We in turn must trust that our mates can handle the whole truth about us; we can't presume that we know better than our companions what information they should hear.

We may think that our private thoughts are none of our mate's business; but remember, relationships aren't business, they're personal.

It's important to discuss with our partners any fears we have about potential problems in the relationship, and to reveal our judgments and suspicions about our mates and why they concern us.

We need to disclose to our partners our past and present limitations or dysfunctional patterns. Our companions may feel threatened or jealous to hear we're attracted to another person; however, if they know we will always tell them everything, then they can trust that we care enough about them, and the relationship, to reveal the whole truth as it unfolds.

We must be willing to be as transparent as possible and offer to answer in complete honesty any questions our mates may have about us, no matter how personal the question or how vulnerable it makes us feel. If we want our mates to be open and honest with us, then we have to set the example by honestly answering their questions.

We must ask them very direct questions—what we truly want to know. If we beat around the bush, our partners will sense we're not being completely vulnerable with our questions or statements. Some examples of direct questions are:

- "At this point in our relationship, what are your greatest doubts about us?"
- "What areas do you have the most difficult time being honest about?"
- "What unhealthy patterns did you have in your past relationships that I should be aware of?"

Below are some statements which reveal to our partners our willingness to be open:

- "In most of my relationships I've had a pattern of being very critical of my mate."

- "I realize now that I wasn't completely honest with you when I said I wanted children."
- "I have a hard time visualizing us still being together five years from now."

All of these statements may be difficult to reveal. However, the openness—the full disclosure—will help to develop the trust that creates friendship in a healthy relationship.

Tip 12

Using Key Words

How many times have we heard a scenario similar to this?

Chris: *"Why didn't you tell me you've been considering a divorce?"*

Pat: *"I've told you many times but you just wouldn't listen."*

Chris: *"When did you tell me?"*

Pat: *"I tell you every time we get into an argument that I'm unhappy with this marriage."*

Chris: *"Saying you're unhappy is far from saying you're thinking of divorce."*

Pat: *"I've tried and tried to tell you that we're in trouble."*

Sound familiar? Many times we're surprised when our companions inform us that what they've been saying to us means much more than what we've heard. It's classic miscommunication and can be damaging if critical issues are present.

One way we can minimize misunderstandings is by learning to establish key words that we can use whenever something important must be communicated. For instance, we can make a pact to say a code phrase such as "I think it's time we need to have *the talk*" should we ever decide we're thinking of splitting up with our partner. This will serve to alert our partners so they won't mistake what we're saying. We could complain for days about how dissatisfied we are with our relationship, but if we don't use the specific phrase "We need to have *the talk*," then nothing we ever say could be *mistaken* to mean we want to break up.

> Key words give us the freedom to fully express ourselves without worrying that our mates will get the wrong message.

Another time to use key words would be when we find ourselves constantly getting into the same type of argument that leads to the same end. Rather than repeating the disagreement, we can work out a code word or phrase that means "Hey, I just realized this is another one of those reactionary ruts that we've gotten into and can't seem to solve at this time." The key word or phrase here could be "Are we back in our rut again?"

For the most part, we don't need to come up with many key words. However, if used judiciously and well they can help us avoid miscommunication that could be detrimental to our relationship.

Tip 13

Communication Contracts

Virginia couldn't believe her ears. Buddy had just told her that he was moving to another state. He'd received a better job offer three months before and had been struggling with the decision to stay or move. Buddy cared about Virginia and saw no reason to worry her if he wasn't going to move, so he didn't mention the possibility until he'd made up his mind.

Virginia was locked into her job, so his decision meant they would have to separate. They'd been dating for eight months, and Virginia had just started to open her heart to him. The news would have been difficult to bear three months earlier, but because of the emotional investments she had recently made and Buddy's concealment of the truth, Virginia was deeply hurt. His abrupt announcement seemed unfair and inconsiderate.

When we think of contracts among couples, we usually think of a written marriage contract to love and honor until irreconcilable differences part us. There are, however, many other contracts in the form of verbal agreements or promises that couples can make to promote security and facilitate trust.

Contracts help to eliminate the false assumptions that can hinder communication. They can be designed by reviewing past conflicts and reaching agreements that will avert or solve potential problems.

Agreements to be monogamous, 100 percent honest with each other, or to seek counseling when the relationship needs help are common contracts that work for many couples. Other contracts include regularly checking in with each other (as in Tip 10) or practicing full disclosure (as in Tip 11).

Good communication is essential to healthy relationships; communication contracts help us to clearly see our responsibility in maintaining those relationships.

A helpful contract for many couples is agreeing to inform each other as soon as possible about any change that could affect the relationship. Change is inherent in all healthy relationships, but not all changes are initiated by both people. Sometimes one person feels a need for something different, or an event occurs—such as Buddy's job offer—that could affect the relationship. It's only fair to inform our companions of potential changes as soon as we are aware of them.

We can make a contract with our mates to avoid making one-sided decisions, or to immediately inform our mates of any change that could have a significant impact on the relationship.

Another good contract that can be made if a relationship is touch and go is for both parties to agree to be fully committed for a set amount of time. During this time, say, one to six months, neither one is to even consider breaking up as an option. This gives both people temporary security and forces them to search for constructive solutions to their problems instead of giving up and separating.

All couples have their own unique issues. It's up to them to discover and then address those issues before they blossom into crises. Designing contracts to meet particular needs is one way to avert major problems.

Tip 14

Avoiding Absolutes

Rich was in a quandary; last month during an argument, he threatened Jane that if she went out at night with her girlfriends again, he wouldn't be home when she returned. Tonight Jane's coworkers invited her to a bachelorette party and Jane went. Now, Rich had to decide if he was going to keep to his word or renege his threat. He didn't want to leave Jane but he also didn't want to look like a fool by backing down on his threat, especially since he had chastised Jane for years about not following through.

Rich wonders how he gets himself in such predicaments. Last week at the office he got into a huge argument with a coworker when he said their boss was never on time.

We often use absolute, extreme, and all-or-nothing statements or behavior to express our boundaries or show how strongly we feel about something, but for the most part this absolute thinking limits us.

Whenever we have to resort to ultimatums, it's a good indicator that our relationship is out of control. It has deteriorated to the point where we don't trust that our partners care enough about our needs to respond to them unless we say or do something drastic. Whenever we do or say something rash, it puts us, and our companions, in a bind because in order to help our credibility we either have to fulfill our promise or back up our extreme statements with evidence.

Absolute words such as *never, always,* and *everybody* are difficult to prove. Absolute statements are just as limiting as either-or statements.

When we resort to using terms such as good or bad, right or wrong, or weak or strong, it reveals our inflexibility and indicates that we're seeing a very limited view of the situation.

When we can only see things one way or another, we don't have enough choices, so we have to resort to drastic measures such as absolutes. Also, much of our communication is heard in the context of what we've said before. If we're in the habit of speaking dramatically—"If you don't like it, you can leave" or "I hate you"—we sound like someone who's always crying wolf. Our partners won't know when we're seriously distressed because they're used to discounting the urgency of our message.

Often, great communicators will even set up their listeners by understating the importance of their information, so that later when they exaggerate, it will be easier to stress an important point.

We need to avoid absolute statements by communicating accurately so that when we have something important to say, our companions will hear the sincerity in our message and respond appropriately.

Tip 15

{ *Reshaping Our Relationships* }

Jason was happily married to Mary, but he was a health buff and was concerned about her recent weight gain. He knew she could lose her excess pounds if she would exercise and change her eating habits. He also knew she didn't have much discipline, so he figured that if he gave her enough encouragement it would give her the motivation she needed to change her behavior. Whenever Jason would see her eating fatty foods he'd remind her how bad it was for her, and when he exercised he'd invite Mary to join him.

Jason believed that he was helping Mary and that his constant support would demonstrate his love for her, but what he didn't realize was that much of Mary's perception of his love for her was based on his attitude toward her whenever they were together. Because of his constant nagging, Mary decided that he didn't accept her the way she was. The problem with Jason's behavior was not only a matter of his lack of acceptance, but also a matter of the time he spent complaining about

Mary's behavior. It was a serious intrusion on the time they had together.

※　　※　　※

We all have issues with our mates, but if we consistently complain about them, then most of their experience of us is one of lack of acceptance.

> We need to be sure that we have many more positive encounters with our mates than we do negative ones.

Just as we plan a vacation or design a business program, we need to shape our relationships. We need to ask ourselves what impressions we're giving our mates. What do our words and behaviors say to our partners about how we feel about them?

After the courtship period with our mates is over and we know they're committed to us, we often become careless about the impression we're presenting to them.

Studies have shown that even up to two years after first meeting someone, we still retain 80 percent of our initial impression of them. This shows not only how important first impressions are, but also that once we get an opinion of someone we may not change it for years. We can take advantage of this by shaping our relationship—that is, establishing up front what kind of person we want to be seen as. If, for instance, we're the type of person who doesn't hug easily or only hugs our closest friends, yet we secretly envy those who can hug many people, we can start reshaping our relationships by hugging the new people we meet. They may be a little taken aback at first to get a hug instead of a handshake, but because they don't know us, they'll assume that hugging is just our way.

And then, from our first hug on, people will expect us to hug them and won't think twice about it—unless we abuse our hugging rights with inappropriate physical behavior.

Just as we can shape our new relationships, we can start reshaping our old ones, one step at a time. How many times have we wanted to be more accepted by a group with which we were involved, so we became friends with each person one by one?

If we want to reshape our current relationships, then we need to think about our behavior every time we're with them. We need to be conscious of the messages we're giving them.

Remember the golden rule: If we want our mate to love us, we need to be sure they feel good about themselves whenever they're around us.

Tip 16

Learning to Listen

Freddy and Tina love each other, but they've been frustrated for quite some time. Most of their disagreements turn into arguments and they both walk away frustrated. They did find, however, that if they both presented their side of the argument written out on paper, they would often reach an agreement. At first they believed it was because when they spelled out their point of view in writing they could present their position more clearly, but this turned out not to be the case. At one stage they decided to take turns reading their papers aloud to each other. While they were a bit closer to reaching an agreement than they would have been without their points of view in writing, their disagreements still went unresolved. So they went back to reading their letters alone.

What Freddy and Tina didn't realize was that their problem wasn't in expressing themselves, but rather in *hearing* each other. When they were alone and read each other's letters, they were able to take the time to "hear" and then think about what the other had to say. When they were together, they were too busy reacting to what was being said to fully perceive each other's points of view.

Many of us will invest our time to learn better ways of expressing our thoughts and feelings, but we're usually not as interested in learning better ways of listening. We know the more efficiently we can communicate, the better we'll be able to convince our mates of our side of an issue; yet we simply don't care as much about learning to hear what our partners have to say.

What we fail to realize is that *listening is 50 percent of communication.* When we communicate with someone that we truly love, we do so in order to fully experience them and their reality, rather than just to fulfill our own needs of expression.

> When we find that we're more interested in what *we* have to say than we are in what our partners are saying, it's an indication that we care more about our feelings than we do about theirs.

This can be a good indicator of our capacity to genuinely love.

In order to be liked, many of us learn to speak well or tell great stories. It's ironic, though, that if we don't learn to listen we'll be perceived by others as bores. At first others may find us interesting, but they soon realize that there's no exchange in the relationship. When we go on and on about ourselves or our ideas, we communicate little interest in others.

People who hear us may learn a few things from us, but they eventually walk away feeling unvalued or feeling a lack of connection. People love to be heard, so if we want them to enjoy our presence, we need to learn to hear *them*.

Many of us communicate by the old shoot-and-reload method: We shoot our message at our partner and then reload our next message while they're talking. We're so busy preparing our rebuttal that we fail to actually hear what our mate is saying.

Even if we've learned to sit quietly and give our full attention without interrupting, there is still much more to being a good listener. We need to learn to listen without reactions such as:

- Rehearsing our rebuttal.
- Defending our position.
- Jumping to conclusions.

- Discounting their message.
- Judging whose position is more fair.
- Guessing their hidden agendas.

Each of these is difficult to do, but we'll never master communication unless we make a conscious commitment to become a good listener and learn to fully engage ourselves when our companion is speaking. Being a good listener requires that we constantly use those three magic words: "Tell me more."

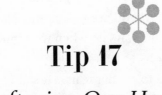

Tip 17

Softening Our Heart

"Me stubborn?" Charles asks Tammy as he becomes even more cool-headed and logical. "I'm just telling you how I see the situation, and then you can tell me how you see it." Tammy starts to cry. "You're distancing yourself like you always do when we argue. I can't feel you; I feel only your walls," she sobs.

Charles is amazed to see her tears. He's always surprised when she gets so sensitive about their simple discussions. Sometimes her tears melt him, other times they only make him cooler, more logical, more defensive. He wonders why he always has to push her to the point of tears before he can let down his emotional walls and soften his heart.

Have you ever noticed that sometimes when you argue with your mate you both are able to reach an agreement, yet at other times things get worse? Have you also noticed that the times when things get worse are the times when you have emotional walls up—walls erected due to being hurt, angry, stubborn, or needing to be right? These walls are all forms of defensiveness. They're all reactions that cause emotional distancing which puts huge barriers between us and our mates.

Often we're midway into a discussion before we become aware of these walls. Even though we know our defenses will hinder us from reaching resolution, we're either too charged to let them down or we don't know how. Why is it that sometimes when our mate cries we get cooler, more logical, and other times their tears soften our stance and we're able to reach an agreement?

With communication skills, we eventually learn to melt our companion's defense mechanisms. However, learning to defuse our own charge, when we have our dander up, requires an entirely different skill.

Learning to soften our heart when we have a strong need to be right, or when we feel attacked, often requires reprogramming a lifetime of automatic responses. However, it is possible to do—first, by understanding why some of us tend to be so rigid and defensive, and second, by learning and practicing two new "inner-action" tools.

Some people tend to operate from a more flexible and gentler position than do others. They tend not to need to be right as often. They are more willing to accept another's point of view, and are more readily willing to apologize when they see they could be wrong. These people are inclined to apologize because, as does acknowledging a gift or a compliment, it creates intimacy.

Others inherently tend to avoid this type of intimacy. They think apologizing, admitting they are wrong, will not only make them less of a person, but will show weakness or cause them to have less bargaining power in future arguments. These people seem to need to have an ongoing perception of themselves as always right, and they need this validated by others. However, these types of people will never *say* that they're always right or that they *never* make mistakes. Nonetheless, they tend to believe that admitting they're wrong to themselves or to others means they're somehow less than they were before. However, they're the only ones who are convinced that—or who even care whether—they're infallible. They believe apologizing would acknowledge that they're not as smart or as competent as they are, or that their intentions aren't as pure as they want themselves or others to believe.

Rather than admit fault, it's easier for them to take a stance on an issue and defend it at all costs, even if it means making excuses or denials, blaming others, or, eventually, avoiding the issue entirely.

Here are a couple of tools that can help to soften our hearts and our behavior:

1. The first tool comes from an old Chinese proverb that suggests saying "thank you" at least twenty times a day, and "I'm sorry" at least ten.

   We can use this every day to start retraining old patterns. Practicing the "thank you" part isn't so hard, but getting used to saying "I'm sorry" at times when we're not used to it takes a bit of courage.

   Once we begin apologizing on a more frequent basis—and the initial feeling of groveling fades away—we soon discover a few surprises. No one will notice initially that we're doing anything different—unless of course we've been a complete jerk.

If we're not used to apologizing, we may expect the recipient of our newfound humility to take immediate advantage of us and our vulnerability. We may fear they'll think that because we're wrong in this one instance, we're wrong about the entire argument. To our surprise, we'll find that this rarely happens.

Another surprise is that we achieve a whole new attitude. We'll find apologizing for something doesn't demean us in any way, and it actually gets us more respect and rapport with others. Others will feel our softness, our openness, and start to feel safe enough to let their defenses down, therefore being less confrontational.

The two difficult parts of this tool are, first, the self-honesty it takes to admit we're wrong, and second, getting the courage to say the initial "I'm sorry" in a situation where we usually wouldn't apologize—situations such as snapping at our mate, or committing minor infractions at work, like interrupting while our colleagues are speaking. Once we see it's normal to apologize, however, it'll be much easier to make it a healthy habit.

2. The second tool involves focusing on feelings, and it can be used in the heat of an argument when we find ourselves being hard or stubborn. Of course there may be many apparently justifiable reasons why we've become defensive, like being blamed, or feeling hurt or insecure. Regardless of the reasons, if we know we're being hard and that our discussion isn't going to get any-

where as long as we have our walls up, then we need to be able to break through ourselves.

Those times when another's tears cause us to become even more logical or defensive may be the times when we have feelings of guilt or regret. They're times when we're so caught up in the issues, or our defenses, that we lose emotional contact with our mate's feelings. Those times when their tears melt us may be the times when we're able to *feel* their feelings more strongly than our own and in spite of our defenses.

This second tool should be used to focus on present feelings, first our mate's and then our own. It's a question of staying with feelings and dropping the issues, forgetting for the present who did what and who wants what. We need to talk about how our mate feels, right then and there, and how we feel about ourselves, about them, and about the present argument. We need to remind our mates that we care more about them and our relationship than we do about any issues that we're dealing with.

Focusing on feelings will force us to access our heart and leave principles, positions, and past problems temporarily on hold until we can come from a more loving, caring, and softer position.

Until we get more in touch with our immediate feelings, being softer may be a challenge. Being so personal and intimate, however, will soften our companion's heart; it will allow the person to connect with us, rather than encounter our walls.

Tip 18

{ *Repatterning Our Reactions* }

Lea woke up feeling especially sensitive on her birthday. She wanted to share some of her feelings with Tom, so while he was shaving she hugged him from behind, pressing her cheek against his back. She hoped they could have a close, intimate connection the entire day. Tom had just put a new blade in his razor, and as he patted Lea's hand, he cut himself. He became angry and blamed Lea for bumping him. Disappointed and hurt, Lea walked away.

Tom made breakfast and then surprised Lea by presenting her with two train tickets out of town that day. Lea had been suggesting they take a train to a symphony for years, but when Tom presented them, her reaction wasn't that enthusiastic. She was still upset about Tom snapping at her earlier.

Tom had rearranged much of his work schedule to make the trip on a Friday, so when Lea seemed ungrateful, he felt hurt. They attended the symphony that evening but the trip was strained and the emotional separation they both felt lasted all day.

Both Tom and Lea want the same closeness in their relationship, but neither knows how to maintain it. They don't know how to be direct and ask for what they want. They both have patterns of *reacting*, rather than *replying*. Reacting is "showing"; it's a nonverbal, indirect attempt to use action to communicate how we feel rather than by "replying," which is verbalizing or stating our thoughts and feelings. Reacting is *doing* something in response to what our partner says or does rather than *talking* to them about it. It is valuing the nonverbal over the verbal, "showing" over "saying."

Other examples of showing instead of saying are when we resort to game playing. Instead of being direct and honest about what we feel or want, we try to manipulate our mates to meet our needs. We say to ourselves, "If they're going to be that way, then I'm going to do *such and such.*" Or we try to teach our partner a lesson: "I'll show them." Or we refuse to answer them when they call us. These are all forms of reacting instead of replying.

Tom and Lea blame each other for how they're feeling. They both are attached to their expectations of each other. When Lea wanted intimacy from Tom, she acted by hugging him, expecting him to read her intentions. When Tom cut himself, he became angry, but instead of realizing that his anger was caused by his inability to deal maturely with his pain, he reacted by blaming Lea. Lea then felt disappointed because her expectations weren't met. Instead of telling (saying to) Tom how she felt, she reacted by walking away (showing him how she felt).

When Tom presented the tickets, he expected Lea to be appreciative of his intentions. When she wasn't, instead of talking to her about it and inquiring as to why she wasn't excited, Tom felt hurt, which was a reaction to her lack of appreciation for the tickets—which was a reaction to his anger at her when he cut himself, which in turn was a reaction to his pain. These reactions boomeranged back and forth all day. Tom reacted to her reaction to his reaction. Instead of talking to each other when they felt hurt, they merely reacted, which caused more pain for both of them. The result: neither of them experienced the emotional connection they had hoped for.

Often we're so involved with thinking about what we've just done, or planning our next move, that we neglect to simply be in the present. If we spent more time in the moment being aware of the source of our thoughts and feelings, we'd realize how much of our lives are dictated by our reactions to others. We continually blame others for how we feel, instead of recognizing that we are the source of all of our own emotions. No one can *make* us angry, sad, or upset—not a slow driver on the freeway, or an overbearing boss, or an unappreciative mate.

> We are the cause of all of our emotions. If we're peaceful and patient internally, nothing anyone ever says or does can disturb us emotionally.

Someone may trigger emotions in us by reactivating our old emotional baggage, but that's our responsibility, not theirs. If we're secure, someone can call us an idiot and it won't hurt our feelings. If we wake up irritable and live our day being impatient with others, we need to repattern our reactions by becoming self-aware. Every time we get angry, we need to say to ourselves, "If I wasn't irritable to begin with, I wouldn't have gotten angry with this situation. I can't blame others even if their actions triggered my impatience."

If we can recognize our reaction patterns, we can change them. We need to reply to our mates rather than react to them. We need to take responsibility for our emotions rather than blame others for them. By repatterning our reactions, we can be proactive rather than reactive.

Tip 19

{ *Comprehensive Communication* }

Randy dated Hanna for a few weeks. He liked her but had no idea how she felt about their relationship. Whenever Randy asked her out she always seemed reluctant; however, after each date she would tell him how much fun she'd had. Hanna never returned his phone calls nor would she initiate them, yet when they dated Hanna was always affectionate and seemed to enjoy his company.

One day Hanna invited Randy to take a two-day drive with her to her sister's wedding. Randy was excited about spending five days with her, but when it came time to rent a motel room Randy was uncertain what to do. He didn't know if Hanna was planning to sleep alone or with him. During their drive, Hanna had opened up to Randy so much he felt closer to her than ever, but because of all the mixed messages he'd received so far he was uncertain what to expect.

Randy didn't want her to feel either pressured or rejected by him. The motel didn't have a room with separate beds, and Randy couldn't afford to pay for two rooms. All he could do was rent one room with a large bed.

When he told Hanna, she became angry and called him presumptuous. She rented her own room and took a taxi to the bus station the next morning. Randy drove home alone.

Hanna and Randy could have avoided their conflict if they had discussed up front how much Hanna was interested in Randy and what their expectations were for the trip. They could have talked about the motel before they left home, and discussed all money issues such as gas, room, and food.

❊   ❊   ❊

The mistakes Randy and Hanna made are obvious now, yet many of us fall short of complete, well-rounded, comprehensive communication. Without good communication role models, we simply aren't accustomed to informing others as often as we should about what we're feeling and thinking. As the saying goes, we don't know what we've got until it's gone. It's also true that we don't know what we've missed until we've experienced it.

> Only in those rare instances when we get a chance to meet a great communicator do we get a sense of how insufficient we've been when relating to others.

Whether this insufficiency is due to a lack of time or a lack of skills, most of us don't communicate as effectively as we could. Our largest problem isn't that we're being impolite or grammatically incorrect, or that we're not getting our message across; our problem is that our message isn't as complete as it could be and that we aren't speaking enough about the topics we should be talking about. *How* something is said is important, but we need to learn to pay attention to *what* is said.

Imagine the stereotypical cowboys of the past, having few words about any situation. Communicating with them was difficult because they simply didn't say enough to inform others completely about any given situation. Although not as extreme, our communications are often not as thorough as they should be.

Below are some examples of when we may not communicate as well as we should.

- As in the example of Hanna and Randy, millions of hearts have been broken because someone didn't ask and someone didn't tell, or because somebody acted on an assumption that wasn't true. We need to address issues before they become problems and learn to assume very little, especially when vulnerable emotions may be involved. We need to constantly check in with our companions and tell them any information we think they may want to know. This form of honesty will protect us as well as them. In most situations, if we're clear with others about what we feel or think, we needn't ever feel responsible for triggering their feelings.

- Good lecturers, it has been said, will tell us what they're going to speak about, then they'll give their speech, and then they'll finish by telling us what they told us. When talking to our mates about an important issue, we need to be just as thorough. We need to set the conversation up by stating the issues we want to discuss. Then after the discussion, we need to state very clearly what decisions were made. This way if something isn't certain, we'll be able to address it then rather than find out later we were in disagreement.

- Sometimes our partners will want to talk when we're busy or they'll mention a topic that we're not interested in. Rather than ignoring them or suggesting we discuss it later, we need to reassure them that if it's important enough for them to mention, then it's important enough for us to acknowledge their interest and to schedule a time to talk.

Comprehensive communication is being complete and thorough in every important communication.

{ **Tip 20**

Walking Our Talk }

Roland and Dawn had read many books on relationships and had taken various self-help classes for years. They were so well-informed, they could have taught workshops on how to have empowering relationships. Yet in spite of how much they knew, their own marriage was unsatisfying.

When they first met, they spent much of their time discussing relationships and communication techniques. They shared their ideas and made contracts with each other so their relationship would be fulfilling and enduring.

As time went by and their schedules became busier, they didn't get to spend the quality time they needed with each other. Their communication began to break down, and an emotional separation resulted. They started to accumulate resentments toward each other because of ongoing problems they were never able to completely resolve.

As they became aware of growing problems, they tried to schedule talks to address their issues. But the quality time they managed to spend together felt so precious that they didn't want to waste it by complaining—so they put off addressing the problems until later. Postponing the discussion of important issues only prolonged their resentment, sending them into a downward cycle that was even more difficult to escape from. Their commitment to each other was so strong they didn't end their relationship, but they also didn't have the relationship they wanted, or the one they knew was possible.

It's been demonstrated many times that we don't always do what we know we could do. Even professionals fail to follow their own advice.

> It's not always a question of what we know, but **whether** we
> are using what we know.

If we know much, we must do much—if we believe in "walking our talk." The key question is: Are we fully integrating what we know into our lives, or is our knowledge only theoretical?

It all boils down to our commitment to happiness and personal growth. Are we willing to settle for a "good enough" relationship, or are we determined to raise our standards higher than what we're used to, or above most of the relationships we've seen?

Remembering all of the tips in this book isn't going to help us have better relationships. But following and practicing these tips will. I've heard acquaintances say that they already knew all of the tips I offered in my first book; yet I constantly see them in difficult situations that could have been avoided or resolved if they had only applied these ideas—that is, if they had "walked their talk."

About the Author

Doyle Barnett left the Ozarks as a teenager to join a Zen monastery. He left the monastery to join the Brotherhood of the Sun, an Eastern spiritual order—founded by a disciple of the famous yogi Paramahansa Yogananda—where he lived and studied for nine years.

Doyle is now a certified master neuro-linguistic programmer (NLP) with the Society of NLP and the Advanced Training Institute. He is also a mediator certified by the Mediation Group, along with the Community Mediation Program of Santa Barbara County. In addition, he's a member of the local Isla Vista Mediation program and the Southern California Mediation Association.

Doyle is certified as a sexual assault counselor at the Santa Barbara Rape Crisis Center. He has maintained a private practice in Santa Barbara that includes NLP training for other professionals in business as well as various human services organizations. He has led groups exploring topics in communication and relation-ships since 1987, and has been a frequent guest speaker on national radio and tele-vision.

Doyle is writing his second screenplay. His works have been published in national magazines and newspapers. Currently, he's finishing his fourth book.

More Communication Tips?

Although most of this book is about the unhealthy behavior of couples, no couple is completely dysfunctional, just as no couple is entirely flawless. We all have lessons we need to learn as well as lessons we can teach. If you or your mate has a communication or relationship tip that has worked well for you (or someone you know) and you would like to share it, please send it to us at:

Doyle Barnett
535 Barker Pass Road
Montecito, CA 93108
Fax (805) 969-3157

If we use your tip in a future volume, we will make sure that you are credited for your submission.

Thanks for playing your part in this learning adventure we call life.

DOYLE BARNETT